COFFEE
CAFÉ

COFFEE
CAFÉ

Sherri Johns

First published in 2005 by New Holland Publishers Ltd
London ■ Cape Town ■ Sydney ■ Auckland
www.newhollandpublishers.com
Copyright © 2005 New Holland Publishers (UK) Ltd

86 Edgware Road
London
W2 2EA
United Kingdom

14 Aquatic Drive
Frenchs Forest
NSW 2086
Australia

80 McKenzie Street
Cape Town
8001
South Africa

218 Lake Road
Northcote
Auckland
New Zealand

ISBN 1 84537 037 6

Publisher: Mariëlle Renssen
Publishing managers: Claudia Dos Santos, Simon Pooley
Commissioning editor: Alfred LeMaitre
Designer: Nathalie Scott
Junior Editor: Nicky Steenkamp
Senior Editor: Anna Tanneberger
Picture researcher: Tamlyn Beaumont-Thomas
Production: Myrna Collins
Barista: Sherri Johns
Stylist: Anke Roux

Reproduction by Unifoto (Pty) Ltd
Printed and bound in Malaysia by TWP SDN. BHD.

2 4 6 8 10 9 7 5 3 1

Contents

Part 1

Introduction

Who and what is involved in the preparation
of coffee? How do you become a *barista*?
Getting to grips with the basics.

Part 2

Coffee Recipes

Part 1

Introduction

Smell the coffee

Romantic, alluring and intoxicating, coffee is the drink of choice for millions. As the second-largest traded commodity in the world, it plays a role in the lives of more than 12 billion people every single day.

People come together over coffee. I believe that, no matter where you are in the world — at your kitchen table, or in an unfamiliar city or country, neighbourhood, restaurant, or café — you can share the joy of a good cup.

Perhaps you are sitting at a window and watching the world go by as your hands cradle the steaming mug and the fresh coffee sends its heady aromas into the air — a few intro-spective moments spent observing a familiar ritual contribute to your enjoyment of life, alone or with friends, even in unfamiliar sur-roundings. Whenever you travel and wherever you go, you have a friend in coffee.

A little history

Coffee originally grew wild in Ethiopia. Legend has it that a herder named Kaldi discovered it while searching for his missing goats. He found them prancing around a bush from which they ate red berries. In the time-honoured tradition of 'what's good for my goats is good enough for me', Kaldi ate some of the fruit and soon he, too, was dancing and frolicking in high spirits.

A passing abbot spied this merry scene and brought some of the coffee berries back to his abbey. There they were dried, roasted and brewed — and *voilà*! No more sleeping during prayers. Heavenly intervention or simply a robust caffeine rush — either way, coffee received rave reviews. From goat herders and monks to the Ottoman Empire, spice traders, growers, the coffee houses of Vienna and the *baristas* of today, each has played an important part in spreading the gospel of coffee!

Now you, too, have the opportunity to explore and delight the senses with hot or cold creations. Let coffee stir your soul.

The root of the matter

There are two main species of coffee: *Coffea robusta* and the *Arabica* bean. The *robusta* is low-growing, fast-producing, inexpensive and not very flavourful. It is generally used in canned or instant coffees and often features as a cheap blender. Commercial–grade coffee roasters blend this bean to reduce costs and increase their yields.

If you've ever pulled into an all-night diner, bellied up to the bar and bought a cup of their house blend, you'll know what I am talking about. You can see through the brew to the bottom of the mug and, against your better judgement, you take a sip. It's harsh, tastes like a wet paper bag, lacks any life and has an unpleasant lingering finish that only a plate of greasy eggs will mask.

Let's move on to a more pleasant coffee experience: *Robusta*'s uptown cousin, the *Arabica* bean. It is grown at higher altitude, from 1600m (around 3500ft) or more, where the elevation produces cool evening temperatures that slow the growth of the plant, allowing complex sugars to develop in the beans. The *Arabica* bean is known to have rich, full-flavour complexities. A hard, expensive bean, it is prized by the specialty coffee industry.

About the trees and the bees

The *Coffea* tree, actually an evergreen shrub, must grow for about five years before it can produce an annual crop that is equal to approximately 450g (15oz) of roasted coffee.

Sweet jasmine-scented flowers become small buds that ripen into the *Coffea* fruit. The colour of the round, hard fruit changes from green to shades of orange and light reds until it ripens fully into deep red. At that moment, the coffee cherry must be hand-picked and processed the same day, because the fruit will overripen if it stays on the vine for longer. Each red cherry is hand-picked at the peak of its ripeness. Since not all coffee cherries ripen at the same time, pickers will often return to the same plant five or six times. There is, however, a more natural process in which the fruit is allowed to dry partially on the vine and is then winnowed from the coffee seed or pit afterwards.

Now imagine a coffee plantation on a hillside where neither truck nor tractor can navigate. A man named Juan Valdez was used to promote the image of a Colombian coffee picker: Valdez and his *burro* (donkey) climb down a

Opposite Coffea *tree branches, heavy with the cherries in which the beans rest.*

steep mountain path, heavily stuffed canvas bags draped on the animals' back. It takes hard toil to produce your steaming espresso!

On a coffee plantation in India I once met Hindi women balancing large sacks on their heads. The trail was steep and rocky and I was compelled to grip a tree branch to maintain my footing while I snapped photos. But the perfectly balanced women smiled at me as they glided past gracefully on bare feet.

Coffee farming is often referred to as a labour of love, because the farmers dedicate themselves to their *Coffea* trees for five years before they see any return on their investment. For that reason, many of them also rely on other crops or even livestock.

Coffee is grown between the Tropics of Capricorn and Cancer, where the equatorial temperatures, altitude, rain, sun, cloud cover and mineral-rich terrain contribute best to the

Above *Only ripe red coffee cherries are hand-picked, one by one.*

flavour of coffee. Microclimates impart a distinctive climatic essence to the coffee as it grows. Much like fine wine, properly brewed coffee will have a flavour profile reflecting its terroir. Processing, roasting and brewing techniques enhance it as well.

The name of the game

Coffee beans are named first for their country of origin, e.g. Sumatra or Kenya. Secondly, they are named for the specific region such as Guatemala Atitlan, or Costa Rica Tarrazu and for the *finca*, *fazenda*, farm or estate from which they hail — e.g. Fazenda Santa Izabel in Brazil, or La Torcaza Estate in Panama.

Once processed, the beans are graded and then sorted by weight, density, colour, visible defects and size. The size of the bean may matter for grading but it is not the determining factor in taste.

Roasting

Roasting is a process by which coffee is cooked in a fluidized bed or drum roaster. The green, uncooked beans bounce and tumble, reflecting heat from the drum walls or each other and pop, much like popcorn. Roast masters carefully monitor the roast degree because, in an instant, the coffee can go from a moderate city roast to a full dark French. Once this happens, there is absolutely no reversing the process — the natural sugars caramelize and come to the surface of the bean as an oily sheen.

Roast degrees are generally region specific. Northern Europeans seem to prefer a rather light roast. As a result their coffee is a medium brown colour. Further south a darker, more robust tint is preferred.

Today there is a renewal of interest in coffee. Cup by cup, the allure of this inky brew, whether laced with steamy milk foam or brandy, is day by day being discovered by a new, appreciative audience. The professional *barista* has a lot to do with this new development.

Left *(Clockwise from bottom left) Parchment beans in a protective outer skin; green, unroasted beans; and dark, roasted beans.*

What is a barista?

A *barista* is a professional 'chef of coffee', who has been trained in the craft of coffee preparation and customer service skills. Italy has the oldest tradition of *baristas*: men and women who prepare hundreds of coffees a day, professionally and effortlessly. The espresso flows seamlessly from *mano* to *macchina* to *mano* all within a few minutes. They are the traditional *baristas*.

The new *barista* is someone who has a passion for coffee and espresso and who finds joy in preparing the perfect cup. These newcomers challenge themselves to do an excellent job on a daily basis and to brew an outstanding cup for each of their customers. They learn about coffee blends and roasts, discover exactly how the coffee should taste and take pride in presenting the perfect espresso!

Baristas challenge themselves to become knowledgeable about where and how coffee is grown. They learn about brewing and grinding equipment until they know it as well as a racing car mechanic knows his engine.

Above *A* barista *is serious about the preparation of good coffee. The first lesson you can learn from the masters is: don't rush it!*

They know when the grinding burrs need replacing and when the pump is acting up. *Baristas* aspire to be creative with coffee. They have fun, but are serious about good coffee preparation.

An important role of the *barista* is to give a face to the coffee. The *barista*'s customers do not visit coffee farms, or know much about how coffee is prepared, but they do know when their favourite *barista* is on duty and they know what to expect. Of the 20 pairs of hands that touch coffee from seed to cup, the *barista*'s is the last — and most important — pair that turns the coffee over to the customer to enjoy.

Those lacklustre individuals who find themselves stuck behind an espresso machine and lack not only training but passion are not *baristas*. They do the specialty coffee industry and the coffee customers no good at all.

Does it take a lifetime to become a *barista*? No, anyone can do it, provided you enjoy your coffee, its challenges and that you want to learn. Even the home-schooled *barista* can create designer drinks with which to impress family and friends. Inspiration for tasty coffee concoctions is easy to find and soon you, too, can brew and blend to your heart's content. There are various interesting sites on the Internet; www.coffeegeek.com is a good place to start. For all you budding *baristas* out there, this book is for you. Let's pour coffee!

Tools of the trade

What will you need to get started? Your kitchen could soon take the shape of the local espresso bar or science lab, if you let it. Let's keep you in an apron rather than a lab coat and begin with the basics. Firstly, if you plan to use espresso in recipes you'll need a good

Below *The right equipment will ensure success and less mess.*

home espresso machine or a small professional one. Alternatively, you might obtain espresso shots from a nearby neighbourhood café, but if you plan to spend a fair amount of time and money on espresso, you might just as well buy a machine for home use.

Do a little research to find out what is available and the performance ratings of each. The home models are just that — home models generally incapable of producing commercially viable quantities, though some are definitely better than others.

If you are really serious about the art of espresso and have the money and the countertop space in your kitchen or bar, you may consider investing in a single group commercial machine for home use. Why? Because nothing beats a freshly ground and brewed espresso as the key ingredient in a signature drink. A single group commercial espresso machine has a porta filter that can steam milk and brew a double shot, or it can make two single espressos at a time. But be warned: you will never have another party at which you are not on bar duty.

One of my funniest party memories concerns the farewell party of a friend — a local TV news reporter moving on to an anchor position at a large network — who had once worked for me as a *barista*.

The party took place at a producer's home where I knew no-one. In the kitchen I spied an old friend, a home espresso machine sitting on the counter, and asked the host how he liked the machine. He groused that he could never get good milk foam. Quickly, I swung into action, asked for a steaming pitcher, filled it with fresh cold milk and a *barista* lesson began. As the host finished his drink other guests lined up to watch and ask questions.

Before I knew it, the entire newscast was there interviewing and asking about coffee. The party had moved into the kitchen and everyone laughed when I put the guest of honour, my friend, on the bar. She began making drinks just as she had in the old days.

I guess the moral of the story is: once a *barista*, always a *barista*.

Espresso Machine — commercial grade or high-end home units available.

Grinder — this machine grinds whole-bean coffee just before brewing. Work with a burr grinder. Burrs are flat blades with several sharp edges that face one another and press or cut the coffee beans as they pass through the beans. The ground coffee is then projected into a chamber, or directly into the porta filter.

A porta filter is the hand-held device that holds ground coffee and fits into the port on the espresso machine. Commercial espresso machine grinders vary in size and price, so ensure you invest in a dependable brand and that the grinder can be easily cleaned.

Small wares — these are small utensils and tools to get your espresso arsenal ready.

Steaming pitchers — you will need two: one small and one medium. Pitchers with a pointed spout are good for creating latte art.

A pitcher with a bell-shaped rim will enable you to pour foam and milk simultaneously. Stainless steel containers are much preferred because they do not break.

Shot glasses — to see the espresso as it pours. This way you can watch the process, look at the swirling crema and know it is a good shot. Get four in case of breakage.

Steaming thermometer — with a large dial, deep spindle and clip to fit snugly onto the rim of the steaming pitcher. This gadget ensures that milk doesn't burn while steaming, assuming you watch the thermometer, of course.

Tamper — okay, bad joke time: no *barista* should EVER lose his tamper. There, I said it.

Hand-held tampers fit snugly into the palm and press ground coffee into the porta filter. They are the diameter of the filter basket. Size depends on the make and model of your espresso machine. Lately, there has been a lot of research on tamper technology — whether it should be flat or concave, made of stainless steel or aluminium. Whatever the outcome, do make certain it feels comfortable and fits into the filter basket of your porta filter.

Knock Box — for spent grounds. This box sits on the counter and is handy for saving all those used espresso grounds for your garden.

Bar towels — one specifically for the steam wand on the espresso machine. Another for counter cleaning and a third for wiping out the porta filter basket. White towels can be bleached. Black shows no trace! The porta filter keeps counters from getting scratched.

Demitasse cups, saucers and spoons — invest in a chic set of barware. It looks beautiful on top of the machine where it will stay warm.

Fancy barware — Do an inventory of what you own. You could use those beautiful hand-blown glasses from your Mexican vacation. Martini glasses fit for a 1940s-themed cocktail hour will do perfectly. Get them off the shelf and dusted. Designer mugs are good for snuggle-worthy morning coffee concoctions.

Serving tray; cocktail shaker; a whipped cream siphon and chargers; tall stir spoons and fancy stir sticks — I think you get the point here: no holds barred. Get creative, have fun and take chances!

Snippets of coffee lore

fun facts and fascinating lore

Fortunes have been made, lost and predicted in coffee. In the Middle East, a *fah* foretells a client's future by reading the coffee grounds, much like a tea leaf reader would. After coffee is drunk, the little cup is carefully turned upside down. The fine silt from the grounds creates trails that are then interpreted. In Malaysia, a prospective groom knows his fate when he is served coffee by a young woman — a sweetened cup indicates acceptance of his proposal, unsweetened means he returns to the bachelors' pool.

Scandinavians have the highest per capita coffee consumption in the world. Perhaps this is the result of three months of winter when the sun barely peeks over the horizon and an equally drastic summer when one can take photographs outside without a flash at four o' clock in the morning.

Whether on the rocks, tall white, short black, walking, or topless (take-away without a lid to cover it); everybody has a preference — but cafés simply serve coffee in paper cups and think no more of it!

On my first trip to Ethiopia I was fascinated by a woman who performed the coffee ceremony. She was shocked to hear that many people simply buy coffee 'to go'. Coffee was meant to be taken slow, over at least an hour — time enough to share news and gossip with friends.

Drunk internationally, and you have to know coffee lingo wherever you go, so here are a few strange terms I discovered on my travels:

The 'double tall, skinny sleeper with whip' may sound like a lanky, undernourished somnambulist who's into S&M, but refers to a caffé latte made with a decaffeinated double espresso, and nonfat milk with whipped cream.

In Hong Kong, a 'flat white' refers to coffee with steamed milk, but no foam.

In America, black coffee is simply that: black coffee — no sugar and no milk. In Japan, black coffee means with sugar, but no milk.

In Italy, ordering coffee in any café or bar will get you an espresso — a small, short *ristretto espresso*. If you order a double espresso, expect to receive two espressos. Do not look for a chair or bar stool. Most bars are simply 'stand up and drink'.

The 'Americano' is a variation that came about as follows: In the 1950s, American tourists in Italy would innocently order coffee and then wince at the intensity of the dark, heart-stopping brew the *baristi* served in miniature cups. Many a *barista* was asked to make the coffee weaker and obliged by adding a shot of hot water (while muttering a disdainful 'Americano' under his breath). Thus a new creation was born — an espresso with hot water to dilute its strength. Not the flavour, just the intensity.

In Scandinavia, an 'Americano' is simply a long shot — extra water is forced through the espresso grounds until the larger cup is filled. This method is not as flavourful as the Italian one.

Caffé Latte, the Number One speciality coffee served in America, does not exist in Italy. (I call them 'espresso with training wheels'.)

In São Paulo, Brazil, you can order a *karioka*, an espresso with a small amount of hot water said to be named for the citizens of Rio (also called *kariokis*) who prefer their coffee this way. This South American speciality is not to be confused with the Japanese entertainment known as *karaoke* — a 'sing-along bar' where the main beverage served is far from coffee!

The perfect cup

espresso, cappuccino, macchiato and more

A good espresso drink begins with a perfect espresso. No matter what you do to it — whether you serve it on ice, with or without steamed milk, flavourings or chocolate, hot or cold, iced or blended — the finished drink will never surpass the original quality of the espresso. No amount of milk, syrup or spices will better it, so be sure to brew with the freshest and highest quality *Arabica* beans.

Coffee is perishable, so buy and brew only what you expect to use in one week. Store the beans in an airtight container, away from heat, light and moisture, but not in the freezer or refrigerator as this robs the coffee of flavour and exposes it to taints. Grind the beans just before you brew.

Perfect espresso is always freshly made from high-quality coffee that has been finely ground and firmly packed into a porta filter. Espresso is viscous. When the pump is activated it should pour out like warm honey streaming off a spoon. The extraction, or brewing, of espresso produces a thick golden or reddish speckled *crema* that floats atop the small amount of liquid. Typically, an espresso is 30ml (1oz) of fluid, brewed and served directly into a preheated demitasse on a saucer, with a little spoon and a small glass of water. Often, carbonated water is served with the espresso to first cleanse the palate so that the customer enjoys the espresso without interference of residual tastes in the mouth. This practice is particularly common in Japan where coffee consumers are noted for their discerning palates.

The golden *crema* or foam on top is the first indicator of quality. The taste should be balanced, caramel and sweet, with hints of spice. It should linger on your tongue for an hour. It should look good, smell good and taste good.

Cappuccino is espresso with equal portions of steamed and foamed or frothed milk, served in a round ceramic cup of about 150ml (5oz). Rich and creamy, it hides the espresso experience beneath a white layer of foamed milk. It is said to have been invented when an Italian monk added frothed milk to his coffee. Named after an honouring the monks' white hoods, a dollop of foam is added to this day.

Just as a bartender develops personal flair in preparing drinks, the *barista*, too, can add flair to his craft: by pouring steamed milk with a spouted pitcher he or she can create designer embellishments such as a rosetta, hearts or tree patterns in the coffee.

There is much debate over what constitutes a true cappuccino and the amount of milk foam versus steamed or heated milk that should be used to make one. Though one ingredient remains standard — the base of every good cappuccino is espresso — everything else seems to be variable and there are interesting regional specialities. Frothed milk is commonly confused with steamed milk, but it is most important that you — as a budding *barista* — prepare the beverage that has been ordered. Here is a little cappuccino glossary to help you on your way:

Classic Cappuccino — one espresso with equal amounts of steamed and foamed milk served in a 150—180ml (5—6oz) cup.

Dry Cappuccino — one espresso with more foam than steamed milk. The espresso is less diluted and has a more intense espresso flavour.

Wet Cappuccino — one espresso with more steamed milk than foam. This creates a milkier version and is less strong.

Double or Doppio Cappuccino — made from two espressos with steamed milk and foam. Not double in size, but double in strength.

Opposite (*Clockwise from the top*) *You see the following selection of cappuccinos: Wet, Dry, Classic and Double (also known as doppio).*

Part 2

Coffee Recipes

Note: Recipes in this book include garnishes that are not always reflected in the photograph

Espresso Romano

Rumour has it that in old Rome, dishwashing facilities were limited. Lemon was believed to disinfect the cup. Its rind was used to rim the glass where germs could linger from one customer to the next, thus Espresso Romano.

1 espresso

Lemon rind

Prepare the freshly drawn espresso into a preheated demitasse.

Rub the rim of the cup with the outer edge of the lemon rind.

Be careful not to use the pith of the peel.

Espresso Ristretto: Ristretto means restricted in Italian. The normal consumed volume of an espresso is 30ml (1oz). About half the volume is expected in espresso ristretto. The *barista* prepares a regular espresso but before it fills 30ml (1oz), the cup is removed or the pump stopped on the espresso machine. This gives a more intense and flavourful espresso.

Espresso con Leche

This drink is perfect for a mid-morning break or late-night refreshment. The rich, sweetened condensed milk tempers the espresso and is laced with semisweet chocolate powder.

1 espresso

A small amount of chocolate powder

A small amount of sweetened condensed milk

Pour the freshly prepared espresso into a preheated demitasse.

Sprinkle with chocolate powder so that the powder floats on top of the espresso. Steam or froth the sweetened condensed milk, then pour a little bit into the espresso from a small steaming pitcher.

Gently shake the pitcher as you pour to create a milk pattern in the sprinkled chocolate for a sweet treat!

Spanish Macchiato

This is a sweet variation on the Espresso con Leche featuring Mexican chocolate. The latter is a combination of sugar, dark chocolate, almond and cinnamon.

1 espresso	Pour the freshly prepared espresso into a preheated demitasse.
A small amount of Mexican chocolate	Steam the chocolate and sweetened condensed milk together.
A small amount of sweetened condensed milk	Pour the mixture from the pitcher into a demitasse, gently shaking the pitcher from side to side as you pour.
	This creates a marbling pattern in espresso and chocolate milk.

Recipe compliments of 2003 and 2004 Canadian *Barista* Champion, second place World *Barista* Champion and 2004 World Latte Art Champion, Sammy Piccolo of Caffé Artigiano, Vancouver, BC, Canada.

Café Cubano

In espresso coffee in Cuba, locals have adopted a tradition of adding refined sugar to ground coffee prior to brewing. This process produces a sweetened cup.

1 ground Arabica espresso

2 tsp sugar

Distribute a sufficient amount of ground Arabica espresso coffee into the port filter, then add sugar on top.

Tamp well and prepare the espresso as usual, brewing in preheated demitasses. The espresso will be frothy and sweet, Cuban style.

Layered Caffé Latte

Espresso and milk offer not only a flavourful treat but also a visual treat. The brown ring of espresso swirls and waves in the milky white layers until a spoon interrupts the bands of colour.

240ml (8oz) milk

1 espresso

Steam milk to 65.5°C (150°F), allow to rest.

Pour the freshly prepared espresso into a small preheated pitcher.

Add steamed milk to a tall glass. Use a spoon to hold back foam while pouring.

Top the milk with a small amount of the foam to the rim of the glass.

Gently pour the espresso into the glass.

Espresso will pour through the foam and settle on top of the milk creating a nice layering effect.

Caffé Mocha

For those who like chocolate, Caffé Mocha is an excellent introduction into the world of espresso coffees . As smooth as rich hot cocoa, with a slight hint of espresso flavour, this drink is perfect for chilly winter mornings or evenings.

240ml (8oz) milk	Steam the milk and set it aside.
15ml (½oz) chocolate syrup	Place the syrup into a tall glass.
1 espresso	Prepare the espresso as usual and add it to the glass.
Chocolate shavings	Mix thoroughly with the chocolate syrup until it dissolves.
Whipped cream	Fill the glass with steamed milk, stir and top with foam or whipped cream.
	Dust with chocolate shavings.

Café Mezzo Mezzo

As the name implies: half and half.

Half brewed coffee Fill a cup or mug halfway with fresh, hot brewed coffee.

Half steamed milk Fill the remainder of the cup slowly with steamed milk.

Café au Lait

It's April and you're in Paris sipping coffee from a bowl. Imagine a sidewalk café and the Eiffel Tower in front of you. Vive le café! Don't forget the croissants!

Dark brewed coffee

Steamed or heated milk

Fill the bowl with equal amounts of coffee and milk.

Hold the bowl with both hands, sip and enjoy.

Affagato

The name always escapes me until I remember, 'ah, forgot, oh'. Served in European cafés and homes alike, no one turns this down.

1 scoop vanilla ice-cream

Scoop the ice-cream into a small elegant dish or glass.

30ml (1oz) double-strength coffee or 30ml (1oz) toddy coffee

Pour the freshly drawn coffee over the top. You may place a chocolate coffee bean on top.

Chocolate coffee bean optional

Simple, elegant and delicious!

Heavenly Shake

If you like chocolate milkshakes, you will love this coffee shake. Easily the most popular cold coffee drink as well as the easiest to prepare.

2 espressos

45ml (1½oz) amaretto syrup

30ml (1oz) chocolate syrup

60–90ml (2–3oz) ice-cream

2 cups crushed ice

Small amount of whipped cream

Small amount of chocolate powder

Mix all the ingredients in a blender until they form a smooth consistency.

Serve in a 360-480ml (12-16oz) glass.

Top the glass with whipped cream and chocolate powder.

Coffee Milkshake

This smooth coffee milkshake is delicious and easy to prepare. Cup rims can be fancy or plain. Serve with straws on a hot summer day.

3 cups vanilla ice-cream

1 cup milk

½ cup chilled toddy coffee

1 tsp vanilla extract

Small amount of whipped cream

Small amount of chocolate sprinkles

Mix all the ingredients in a blender until smoothly blended.

Serve in a tall glass with a small amount of whipped cream.

Decorate with whipped cream and chocolate sprinkles.

Hazelnut Granita

A perfect dessert of glacé coffee, as refreshing as it is satisfying. Bring out the martini shaker and get into the swing of things. Serve with small chocolates for an elegant final touch.

120ml (4oz) hazelnut syrup

60ml (2oz) toddy coffee or espresso

180ml (6oz) filtered water

2 cups coffee ice cubes

Add all the ingredients into a martini shaker and shake for 45 seconds.

Serve in a chilled glass.

Recipe compliments of Filtron, Huntington Beach, CA, USA

Java Chocolate Shake

Ice-cream, chocolate and coffee are three
of my favourite foods. Blend all together for
a rich, yummy treat. For a dramatic touch,
decorate the interior of the glasses with
chocolate swirls before adding the shake.

**30ml (1oz) toddy coffee
or espresso**

**90ml (3oz) filtered
water**

**30ml (1oz) milk
chocolate bar**

2ℓ vanilla ice-cream

Blend the coffee, filtered water, and the
chocolate bar until all are finely chopped.
Add the softened ice-cream and blend
until smooth.

Recipe compliments of Filtron, Huntington Beach, CA, USA.

Coconut Zesta

I first tasted this drink while judging the US *barista* competition. I was so impressed with the combination of balance and flavours that I remembered it long after the event.

180ml (6oz) coconut milk	Combine the milks and steam or heat it in a saucepan.
180ml (6oz) milk	Dust the rim of the cup with raw sugar.
2 tbsp raw sugar	Brew the espresso directly in a preheated cappuccino cup.
1 espresso	Add raw sugar into the espresso or milk and stir until it dissolves.
1 lime	
2 lime leaves	Pour the steamed or heated milk into the espresso and top it with a zest of lime.
	Snap the lime leaves to release aromatics and garnish on a saucer.

Recipe compliments of *barista* Phuong Tran, second place 2004 USBC, first place North-west *Barista* Jam, Lava Java Café, Ridgefield, WA, USA

The Blueberry

This drink has a unique flavour with a delightful finish. An elegant drink and also delicious.

½ tsp cinnamon

1 tbsp honey

6 espressos

½ cup heavy whipped cream

1 cup frozen blueberries

1 bar dark chocolate

1 whole cinnamon stick

Add the cinnamon and honey to a cocktail shaker. Prepare six shots of espresso. Add the espresso to the cocktail shaker and gently stir with a long whisk when combining it with the cinnamon and honey. Divide the heavy whipped cream into four 60ml (2oz) serving vessels (preferably glass), filling them all halfway. You may garnish with grated cinnamon. Add frozen blueberries to the cocktail shaker and shake seven times. Pour the espresso mixture over the cream, filling each serving vessel ¾ full. Garnish with dark chocolate and cinnamon stick, then serve.

Recipe compliments of *barista* Kyle Larson, 2004 Northwest Regional Champion, Zoka Coffee Roaster & Tea Company, Seattle, WA USA

Viennese Coffee

Soft cream greets your lips as the orange essence tickles your nose. Wintertime coffees are a welcomed reward for guests who brave the cold for a visit.

120ml (4oz) semi-sweet chocolate	Melt chocolate in a heavy saucepan over low heat.
1 tsp sugar	Stir in sugar and whipping cream.
½ cup whipping cream	Blend coffee with a wire whisk, half a cup at a time.
4 cups hot strong coffee	Continue to blend until creamy.
Whipped cream	Top with a dollop of whipped cream and grated orange rind.
Orange rind	

Kaffee mit Schlag

Enjoy this alone or with friends near a fire or a cold, rainy window. Rich — but not over the top for the coffee snob. Simple, clear glass mugs are best to showcase this coffee.

Strong brewed hot coffee	Fill the glass with coffee.
Fresh whipped cream	Top it with a portion of whipped cream.
Cinnamon stick or chocolate swirls	Garnish with a cinnamon stick or shaved chocolate swirls.

Dutch Coffee

I first made this at a coffee house in San Francisco. Something about butter floating in coffee and a cinnamon stick made it seem exotic as a special occasion beverage.

1 cup strong brewed coffee	Blend coffee and cream in a saucepan. Pour mixture into a mug.
½ cup cream	Take cinnamon stick and dip it in butter.
Cinnamon stick	Lay the cinnamon stick flat across the coffee surface and the rim of the mug.
Small pat of butter	The cinnamon stick will float as the butter melts.

Caffé Borgia

The Borgias were a powerful family who used poison masked in coffee and orange to get rid of their enemies. This drink is named after them.

1 cup double-strength hot coffee	Mix the double-strength hot coffee and Mexican chocolate and stir until the chocolate is dissolved.
1 tsp Mexican chocolate powder	
	Add whipped cream.
Small amount of whipped cream	Garnish with orange rind.
Orange rind	

Coconut Crème Café

Sweet, creamy and tropical, Coconut Crème Café is a dessert coffee designed to satisfy the most nit-picking guests. A welcome refreshment after a spicy meal.

30ml (1oz) toddy coffee

½tsp rum or Kahlua extract

150ml (5oz) water

2 tbsp cream coconut

2 tbsp whipping cream

Coconut flakes

Place all ingredients in a blender and blend for 10 seconds until smooth.

Pour mixture into chilled glasses.

Garnish with whipped cream and coconut flakes.

Recipe compliments of Filtron, Huntington Beach, CA, USA

Coffee ice cubes

Ice cubes are placed in drinks to cool them. As the drink cools, the ice melts, diluting the beverage. I prepare many iced drinks with coffee ice cubes. For this, you will need an ice tray or two that you will use only for coffee ice — coffee is strong and will taint the plastic, so when re-used for making cubes with water, they will taste of coffee. Once a coffee ice cube tray, always a coffee ice cube tray!

Trays may be filled with brewed coffee or espresso shots — one per square. Freezing coffee and cream for a light brown cube adds flavour and looks fascinating as the cube melts, leaving a marbling pattern in the glass.

All reference to ice cubes in this section indicates coffee ice cubes, unless otherwise stated. To make the cubes, I recommend a high-quality specialty coffee, Mexican or Brazilian, or a pleasant blend of coffee not roasted too dark. Avoid really strong coffee-flavoured profiles as they may compete with the drink itself.

Simple syrup is my preferred method of sweetening chilled coffee and espresso beverages. The syrup is more effective, since granulated sugar does not dissolve in cold drinks. To make it, take a cup of granulated sugar and dissolve with two cups of water just off the boil. Stir it briskly with a wire whip until the sugar dissolves completely. Store in a pour bottle in the refrigerator until ready for use.

Iced Coffee Americano

An Americano lets you enjoy the full flavour of espresso without the intensity. It is brewed fresh for each person (a rare treat in restaurants). The iced Americano is the chilled version.

Coffee ice cubes

300ml (10oz) filtered water

2 espressos

Simple syrup (optional)

Fill a tall glass with coffee ice cubes and pour in the chilled filtered ice water.

Add the espresso and stir.

Simple syrup may be served on the side.

Make the drink according to your taste by adding more or less espresso.

The Iced Coffee Americano is a great way to enjoy a fresh cup of iced coffee from an espresso machine. This is my favourite iced espresso drink.

Iced Coffee

Refreshing on a hot morning at the office or a lazy afternoon by the pool. This icy beverage is the counterpart of iced tea with a kick.

Fresh Arabica coffee (enough to fill your brewer basket to twice the normal amount)

8 cups of filtered water

1 glass coffee ice cubes

Simple syrup (optional)

Brew double-strength coffee in a press pot or drip brewer. This is simply coffee that is brewed with twice the normal amount that you regularly use. Remember that the brew basket must be able to hold the desired amount of coffee or it will overflow. Remove brewed coffee from the hot plate on the brewer (if brewed on an electric brewer). Allow brewed double-strength coffee to cool at room temperature. Stir and serve in a tall glass filled with coffee ice cubes. Simple syrup may be served on the side.

Toddy Coffee

Toddy is not a very common brewing method although it is catching on. It is sweet and rich. The cold-water brewing method retains body and the natural oils in coffee. The acidity is lessened while the coffee flavour is left intact.

30ml (1oz) coarse ground coffee

4.5ℓ filtered water

If using a toddy maker, make sure your filter comes with it. The filters are round discs of wool or synthetic fibre that are clean and free of foul odours. This method greatly reduces the brightness of the coffee, so start with a coffee that can stand up to the process, e.g. a Vienna blend or darker roasted coffee. My friend, Katy, used to brew Toddy with an African Sanani, which has a deep cherry flavour that would come out in the toddy process. Add a splash of cream. Here, I would not recommend coffee ice cubes.

Iced Caffé Latte

So far, chilled coffees have been made with three variations: brewed double-strength coffee, espresso and toddy. For preparing iced espresso drinks, the order in which ingredients are added is critical.

180ml (6oz) cold milk

2 espressos

Coffee ice cubes

Pour cold milk into a glass of your choice. Add the espresso and mix. Add ice to fill cup. The espresso will dilute if poured onto ice directly. To maintain the integrity of the espresso flavour, use milk first, then espresso, then ice. An iced caffé latte is sometimes called 'on the rocks'. Some people place foamed milk on iced drinks, but it may dilute the flavour. Coffee flavour may be more or less, depending on what type of milk is used. For almond iced latte, add the syrup and change the order: syrup, espresso, cold milk, ice.

Classic Iced Caffé Mocha

For anyone who says they do not enjoy iced coffee. Chocoholics and coffee connoisseurs alike will clamour for more.

Chocolate syrup

2 espressos (or may substitute chilled double-strength coffee)

180ml (6oz) cold milk

½ cup coffee ice cubes

Whipped cream (optional)

Use syrup doodles to create a pattern inside the glass before pouring any liquid into it.

Place chocolate syrup in a pint glass.

Add espresso and mix thoroughly.

Pour cold milk halfway, then fill the rest of the glass to the top with ice.

Some people like whipped cream on this. Be careful of adding whipped cream once the coffee is stirred. The cream separates into clumps, affecting the appearance.

Chocolate syrup may be swirled on top of the cream to finish off.

Banana Chocolate Cooler

I never knew this combination of flavours could be so delicious. Prepare by the blenderful, as friends and family will line up for refills.

1 ripe banana

1 cup chocolate ice-cream

30ml (1oz) toddy coffee

90ml (3oz) filtered water

1 cup coffee ice cubes

Sugar sprinkles

Place all the ingredients in a blender and blend until smooth.

Serve in a tall glass.

Garnish with a banana slice.

Recipe compliments of Filtron, Huntington Beach, California, USA.

Peach Smoothie

Another blended drink that proved to be the hit of the photo shoot. The peach smoothie was elected house favourite by those who did not even drink coffee!

1 cup cream

60ml (2oz) toddy coffee

2 tbsp sugar

1 cup coffee ice cubes

1 cup frozen peaches

1 peach slice

Place all the ingredients in a blender and blend until smooth.

Pour into chilled long glasses.

Recipe compliments of Filtron, Huntington Beach, California, USA.

Espresso Spritz

The simplest sparkling espresso drink ever! You can now make your own bottled espresso drink. It's fresh and easy!

1 espresso	Add the espresso to the sparkling water, then add ice.
60ml (2oz) sparkling water	Rub the rim of the glass with a lemon wedge, then place the wedge on the rim.
A few ice cubes	Alternative preparation: add the espresso to chilled sparkling water, stir and serve.
1 lemon wedge	

Ice-espresso

'This is like candy,' says Fritz Storm, who makes it for his customers and friends alike. I agree, it is an extravagant taste sensation complementing any meal.

1 cup vanilla ice-cream

1 or 2 espressos

Whipped cream

Melt the ice-cream and put it into the whipped cream siphon. Add two gas cartridges. This changes the ice-cream to a consistency you would normally have in whipped cream. Make one espresso or a double. Put a little mountain of ice-cream from the siphon on top of the espresso. Add a small amount of whipped cream, if desired.

Please note: for this you will need a whipped cream siphon that can handle two gas cartridges.

Recipe compliments of Fritz Storm, World Champion *Barista* 2002, Denmark.

Thai Iced Coffee

Surprisingly, this is a concoction of spices and coffee that complement each another. The cardamom spice kicks it up a bit and leaves a pleasant aftertaste.

6 tbsp freshly fine-ground specialty coffee

¼ tsp ground coriander powder

4 or 5 whole green cardamom pods, ground

8 ice cubes

30ml (1oz) heavy whipped cream

Place the coffee and spices in the filter cone of the brewer. (The spices will taint the filter basket, so use one for Thai iced coffee only, or use a paper filter and wash the brew basket thoroughly after each use.) Brew coffee as usual and allow to cool.

Add simple syrup to a tall glass. Add 8 ice cubes and pour coffee 2.5cm (1in) from the top of the glass. Hold the back of a spoon over the glass, slowly pour the heavy whipped cream over the spoon onto the coffee, creating a layered look. This will prevent the cream from dispersing into the coffee right away. Serve with a flexible straw and a tall spoon.

Iced Mint Java

Coffee ice cubes maintain the coffee flavour while the mint leaf adds an aromatic flair. Served in chilled tall glasses accented with green straws, if desired.

Coffee ice cubes

Chilled double-strength coffee

Mint syrup

A small amount of chilled whipped cream

A sprig of fresh mint leaves

Fill a tall glass with coffee ice cubes.

Fill the rest of the glass with chilled coffee. Add a dash of mint syrup and stir well.

Top with a dollop of chilled, whipped cream to taste.

Garnish your drink with a fresh mint sprig and flexible straw.

Black Forest

The flavours of chocolate, cherry, coffee and cream make for a beautiful drink that tastes like its dessert namesake, 'Black Forest Cake'.

30ml (1oz) chocolate syrup

30ml (1oz) toasted marshmallow syrup or whipped cream

15ml (½oz) grenadine

180ml (6oz) chilled toddy coffee

Mix the syrups and grenadine together in a martini glass.

Add chilled coffee.

Gently spoon the whipped cream onto the drink.

Spiral a toothpick through the drink to make patterns.

Be sure to wipe the toothpick each time to ensure a distinct design.

Classic Coffee Float

Soda shops of the 1950s probably never served this. If they had, more adults might have hung around. It's simply chilled coffee and ice-cream served in a tall glass.

180ml (6oz) chilled coffee

1 scoop vanilla ice-cream

Fill a pint-size glass with the chilled coffee. Add a scoop of ice-cream. Balance it on the rim of the glass if you can!

Vietnamese Iced Coffee

After a spicy meal of Vietnamese food, I enjoy this form of coffee. It is sweet and freshly made each time, using a special coffee press.

Vietnamese coffee press

2–4 tbsp finely ground dark roast coffee

2–4 tbsp sweetened condensed milk

2 cups boiling water

1 glass coffee ice cubes

Place ground coffee in Vietnamese coffee press and screw lid down. Put the sweetened condensed milk in the bottom of a coffee cup and set the coffee maker on the rim. Pour boiling water over the screw lid of the press. Adjust tension on the screw lid until bubbles appear through the water, and the coffee drips slowly out the bottom of the press. When all water has dripped through, stir the milk and coffee together. You can drink it warm or try it over ice. If you can't find a Vietnamese coffee press, regular strength espresso is an adequate substitute.

Vanilla Iced Coffee

Sweet, tall and as refreshing as coffee gets. Vanilla flavour adds a little sweetness to the cup and tempers it somewhat for those who enjoy sugar in their brew.

Coffee ice cubes

1 cup chilled toddy coffee

1 tsp vanilla

1 cup milk (can substitute with soymilk, organic, full cream, etc.)

Fill a tall glass with ice.

Add the chilled toddy coffee, vanilla and milk.

Stir and serve.

Caffè Calabrese

Sammy forgot his chocolate discs. He called
his wife on the mobile phone, panic-stricken.
She arrived, the discs in hand, and a winning
signature drink was served.

30ml (1oz) orange-infused caramel

60ml (2oz) toasted almond chantilly cream

1 dark fleur de cacao chocolate disc

45ml (¾oz) filtered water added to 15ml (½oz) ristretto espresso

Pour orange-infused caramel in a glass.
Slowly pour in toasted almond chantilly to
create two layers.

Place chocolate disc on the mixture.

Slowly pour water and espresso mixture on
top of the chocolate disc.

The layers, assembled in a martini glass,
make a beautiful drink.

Recipe compliments of Sammy Piccolo, 2003 and 2004 Canadian *Barista* Champion and
2004 World Latte Art Champion, Caffé Artigiano, Vancouver, BC, Canada.

Cocoa Mocha Mint

This delectable drink is a hit for those who crave chocolate and mint. An ideal steamy concoction for cold winter nights.

30ml (1oz) brandy extract

150ml (5oz) hot chocolate (already made with milk)

30ml (1oz) toddy coffee

15ml (½oz) mint extract

Mix and preheat all the ingredients. Pour into a coffee mug and serve.

May be served hot or cold.

If cold, serve in a long glass with coffee ice cubes.

Recipe compliments of Filtron, Huntington Beach, CA, USA.

Marochino

This is a medium-temperature drink meant to be enjoyed in one sip. The bittersweet chocolate stands up to the intensity of espresso.

1 tsp bitter chocolate sauce	Place chocolate in small glass.
	Add the espresso.
2 espressos	Pour in the steamed milk, while trying to make some latte art on the top.
1 cup milk	

Recipe compliments of Fritz Storm, 2002 World *Barista* Champion, Denmark.

Hearts Aflame

Baristas determine what ingredients are combined together to present new taste sensations. This *barista* loves chocolate and coffee, and is a romantic at heart.

1 chocolate bar

15ml (½oz) cinnamon syrup

15ml (½oz) raspberry syrup

2 hot espressos or 60ml (2oz) hot double-strength brewed coffee

1 cup steam milk

Whipped cream

Blend the chocolate bar, syrups and coffee together.

Add steamed milk.

Garnish with whipped cream and cinnamon sprinkles if desired.

Recipe compliments of *barista* Stefanie Raymond of *Barista*'s Daily Grind, Kearney, Nebraska, USA.

Amoré

A simple and elegant drink, in tall fluted glasses or wide-brimmed stems. The chocolate-dipped strawberry adds a touch of glamour and sweetness to the coffee.

1 cup hot brewed coffee or espresso

Pour in hot coffee.

Slice strawberry and place on glass rim.

1 chocolate-dipped strawberry

Serve on a tray that is decorated with rose petals.

Rose petals (optional)

Recipe compliments of Coffee People, Portland, Oregon USA.

Chilled Island Coffee

Ideal for Sunday brunches with a Hawaiian flair. Guests will feel special as they indulge in chilled coffee sweetened with coconut milk.

Coffee ice cubes

1 cup chilled toddy coffee

Dash of coconut milk

Fill tall glass with ice, then add the chilled toddy coffee.

Add a dash of coconut milk.

The White-Cin

A combination of white chocolate sauce and cinnamon!

30ml (1oz) espresso	Place espresso, cold milk and white chocolate sauce into martini shaker with 6 ice cubes.
30ml (1oz) cold milk	
120ml (4oz) white chocolate sauce	Shake for 45 seconds.
	Pour into chilled wine glasses.
6 ice cubes	Top with a layer of cinnamon powder and white chocolate shavings.
Cinnamon powder	
Small amount of white chocolate shavings	Garnish with a cinnamon stick.
Cinnamon stick	

Recipe compliments of *barista* Joe Hayek, 2002 Lebanese *Barista* Champion, Casper and Gambini's, Beirut, Lebanon.

Mocha After Eight

This beverage can be served up in a designer mug or layered for visual effect in a tall clear glass. Most delicious and enticing.

30ml (1oz) fresh espresso

30ml (1oz) mint syrup

1tbsp chocolate powder

1 cup steamed milk

Fresh mint leaf

Blend coffee, syrup and chocolate powder in preheated cups.

Add the steamed milk.

Garnish with chocolate powder and a fresh mint leaf.

Recipe compliments of *barista* Joe Hayek, 2002 Lebanese *Barista* Champion, Casper and Gambini's, Beirut, Lebanon.

Monk's Cappuccino

A little brandy livens up this coffee classic, which can be made with espresso or hot, concentrated coffee.

60ml (2oz) toddy coffee

⅔ cup hot milk

1 tbsp brandy extract

1 tsp sugar

2 tbsp white chocolate syrup

Whipped cream and chocolate shavings

Place all the ingredients in a blender and blend until smooth.

Pour the drink into a glass and garnish with whipped cream and chocolate shavings.

Summer Sun

A sweet summertime treat is presented by this *barista* as an alternative to regular iced coffee. Can be shaken and poured into freezer-cold glasses for a frosty effect.

30ml (1oz) espresso or toddy coffee

15ml (½oz) butterscotch

1 tsp honey

15ml (½oz) caramel

Mix all ingredients together.

Pour into chilled long glasses.

Serve with honey stick straws.

Recipe compliments of *barista* Stefanie Raymond, *Barista* Daily Grind, Kearny, Nebraska, USA.

Budding Rose

Any flavour may be used for this drink. The colour will change as the flavours do. It's an attractive drink, with alcohol-enhanced pizzazz. Not for the faint of heart!

60ml (2oz) tequila

300ml (10oz) milk or cream

90ml (3oz) strawberry syrup (cherry, blackberry, raspberry)

Ice cubes

30ml (1oz) espresso or toddy coffee

Pour tequila, milk and strawberry syrup over ice cubes into a chilled long glass or pint glass.

Add the espresso or toddy coffee.

Insert a flexible straw.

Serve chilled, iced or at room temperature.

The colours of the milk, red syrup and espresso will marble when the straw is inserted.

Recipe compliments of Coffee People, Portland, Oregon, USA

Caffé Napoli

Small and delicious, this drink can be enjoyed after a meal or by the fireside — sweet treats and coffee all in one sip!

¼ **cup sweetened condensed milk**

1½ **tbsp toasted hazelnut oil**

1 **dash fresh cinnamon**

1 **dash freshly ground cardamom**

360ml (12oz) **full cream milk**

120ml (4oz) **fresh espresso or double-strength coffee**

1 **bar dark chocolate**

Combine the sweetened condensed milk, hazelnut oil, cinnamon and cardamom in a small mixing bowl and whisk. Place the bowl in hot water to keep it warm. Heat the full cream milk on the stove top (without scalding), set it aside for a while, then whisk. Prepare four shots of espresso, pouring each into a 75ml (1½oz) demitasse. You may substitute the espresso with freshly brewed double-strength coffee. Add the sweetened condensed milk blend to each demitasse, followed by the whisked steamed milk. Garnish with dark chocolate and serve.

Recipe compliments of Kyle Larson, 2004 Northwest Regional *Barista* Champion, Zoka Coffee Roaster and Tea Company, Seattle, Washington, USA.

Mexican Mocha

Chocolate is blended with complementary spices and traditionally served this way. We add coffee or espresso and viola for instant results. A most delicious, satisfying drink.

60ml (2oz) milk

2 cups hot double-strength brewed coffee

1 tbsp chocolate syrup

Pinch of cinnamon and cloves

1 chocolate cinnamon stick

Heat the milk, coffee, chocolate syrup and spices together on the stove.

Pour into mugs and garnish with chocolate cinnamon sticks.

Turkish Style Coffee

'*Turk Kavase*' is commonly consumed on every street corner in Istanbul. With this improvised recipe you can enjoy the flavours of Turkey without leaving your kitchen!

1 cup ground dark roast coffee

1 tbsp ground cardamom

8 cups water

¾ cup sugar

Combine coffee and cardamom in a brewer filter basket.

Brew coffee as usual.

Whisk in sugar.

Serve in a small preheated demitasse.

You may add whole cardamom pods to float for a visual effect.

Ginger Snap Macchiato

This tasty and attractive combination melds nicely as a designer drink. It has style, taste and texture.

½ tbsp molasses	Add molasses and caramel into a wide-brim demitasse.
¼ tsp caramel	
Pinch ground ginger	Sprinkle ground ginger.
30ml (1oz) espresso	Add the espresso slowly to save the crema on top.
Pinch ground cinnamon	Sprinkle cinnamon.
½ cup steamed milk	Carefully pour steamed milk over the velvet texture, creating latte art.

Recipe compliments of *barista* Teri Bryany, Black Drop Coffee House, Bellingham, WA, USA

The Marquis

Several spices are combined here to create a complex-flavoured drink that has style, class and balance. I enjoy it as a rainy day pick-me-up.

7.5ml (¼oz) cinnamon syrup

15ml (½oz) vanilla syrup

30ml (1oz) espresso or strong brewed coffee

Pinch ground chicory

Pinch ground cinnamon

Pinch brown sugar

½ cup milk

Pour cinnamon and vanilla syrup into cup.

Brew espresso or coffee with chicory.

Pour syrup from cup and mix well.

Add cinnamon and brown sugar; allow it to melt undisturbed.

Steam or heat milk on stove and stir so that it does not burn.

Slowly pour steamed milk over mixture to make your latte art.

Please note: if brewing espresso with chicory, dose the grounds half-full, add chicory, complete the dose, and tamp at 18.2g (40 lb) of pressure. Chicory, if not completely 'sealed' by the espresso puck, will channel as it extracts into the cup.

Recipe compliments of US *barista* Championship Judge: Alexarc Mastema, The Black Drop Coffeehouse, Bellingham, Washington, USA.

Naked Verbena

Refreshing as it is unique. This *barista* conjured up this beverage while living in Southern California where verbena plants sometimes grow wild.

6 cups of ice cubes

¼ lemon wedge

12 lemon verbena leaves

120ml (4oz) simple syrup (equal parts sugar and water)

8 shots espresso or 240ml (8oz) toddy coffee

The peel of one lemon divided into 4

Combine four cups of ice with the quartered lemon wedges and eight lemon verbena leaves. Squeeze the juice of the lemons onto the verbena leaves and then freeze the ice mixture. Once the ice mixture is frozen, divide it between four martini glasses. Pour 30ml (1oz) of simple syrup onto the ice in each glass. Prepare fresh shots of espresso and pour into a martini shaker with the lemon rind and the remaining four lemon verbena leaves. Add remaining two cups of ice and shake vigorously. Pour evenly into the four glasses. Garnish with a curled lemon peel.

Recipe compliments of Heather Perry, 2003 Western Regional *Barista* Champion, 2003 US *Barista* Champion, Coffee Klatch, San Dimas, California, USA.

Vanilla Mint

Energizing as it is tasty, vanilla mint will temper any hot day. This is an easy drink to prepare. Especially for those who think coffee should be hot to be enjoyed.

30ml (½oz) vanilla

7.5ml (¼oz) crème de menthe

60ml (1oz) espresso or toddy coffee

Coffee ice cubes

Spearmint sprigs

Pour vanilla, crème de menthe and espresso over the coffee ice cubes.

Garnish with spearmint sprigs and add a green straw.

Recipe compliments of *barista* Stefanie Raymond, *Barista*'s Daily Grind, Kearney, Nebraska, USA.

Spanish Coffee

A quintessential after-dinner drink. Practice can make this drink preparation a floor show, particularly if you pour the rum and Kahlua from an arm's distance.

Dash 151 proof rum

Dash Triple Sec

1 shot Kahlua

30ml (1oz) hot coffee

Fresh whipped cream

Nutmeg

Dip the cocktail glass rim in water and then sugar to make a rim of sweetness.

Add a splash of 151 proof rum and Triple Sec. If you're daring, set the glass ablaze. As the flame burns, add one shot of Kahlua. Fill the glass with hot coffee, leaving a small amount of room for fresh whipped cream. Garnish with nutmeg.

HINT: Irish coffee glasses make good vessels for this drink. Practise pouring with alcohol bottles filled with water. It can save on expenses and a spill will not be as devastating as spilling 151 proof! Keep a fire extinguisher nearby.

Jamaica Good Coffee, Mon

To the beat of Rastafarian music, we all had fun with this recipe. It is a slightly sweetened drink that can be made with regular or espresso coffee.

15ml (1oz) caramel

15ml (1oz) Amaretto

60ml (2oz) espresso or double-strength coffee

½ cup milk or coconut milk

Green sugar sprinkles

Place caramel, Amaretto and espresso or freshly brewed double-strength coffee in a mug.

Steam milk or coconut milk on a hot stove without scalding.

Add this to the brew in the mug.

Top with green sugar sprinkles.

Recipe compliments of Danny Johns, WholeCup Coffee Consulting, *Barista* Trainer, US and International *Barista* Event Coordinator, Portland, Oregon, USA.

The Grasshopper

The bright green makes this a perfect Saint Patrick's Day coffee drink! Guests will ask for the recipe.

15ml (½oz) vanilla syrup	Add syrup and crème de menthe to espresso and mix well.
7.5ml (¼oz) crème de menthe	Pour into a cordial glass.
	Top it up with whipped cream.
60ml (2oz) espresso	Crush the spearmint candies and sprinkle on top.
Whipped cream	
Spearmint candies	

Caribbean Coffee

Coffee with a jolt has never tasted so good. This combination of liquors is enhanced by the rich brewed coffee and cream.

30ml (1oz) Tia Maria

30ml (1oz) Jamaican rum (brown)

Sugar or simple syrup

60ml (2oz) espresso or hot double-strength coffee

Whipped cream

Combine Tia Maria, rum and sugar/simple syrup in a small saucepan.

Add the espresso or strong coffee and mix well over heat.

Pour into a 150ml (5oz) or 180ml (6oz) cappuccino cup.

Top with whipped cream.

Mocha with a Kick

Draw attention to detail and woo a lucky recipient with these beautiful patterns. Create concentric circles of chocolate over the cream and drag a toothpick through the rings.

30ml (1oz) crème de cacao

30ml (1oz) Kahlua

Double-strength brewed coffee

Whipped cream

Brown sugar

Combine crème de cacao and Kahlua in a coffee mug.

Add coffee and mix well.

Top with whipped cream and dust with brown sugar.

Amaretto Coffee

Amaretto brings me back to holiday time and long talks by the warm cozy fire. This is a simple brew that can warm up the coldest of nights.

Cinnamon sugar	Moisten the rim of the glass and dip in cinnamon sugar.
30ml (1oz) brandy	Add the brandy and Amaretto.
30ml (1oz) Amaretto	Fill the glass with freshly brewed coffee.
Hot double-strength brewed coffee	Top with whipped cream, toasted almond slices and a cherry, if desired.
Whipped cream	
Toasted almond slices	
Cherries	

Coffee Cachaça

On a recent trip to Brazil, I discovered Cachaça. Wow, my taste buds will never be the same again! Try it here with coffee to temper the strength.

1 shot Brazilian Cachaça	Preheat a glass in hot water.
1 shot Kahlua	Pour in one shot of Brazilian Cachaça, then one shot of Kahlua.
90ml (3oz) hot coffee	Add 90ml (3oz) freshly brewed hot coffee and sugar.
Sugar	Carefully pour the whipped cream.
Small amount of whipped cream	Garnish with a strawberry, mint cookie and mint leaves.
1 Strawberry	
1 mint cookie	
Mint leaves	

Cajun Coffee

Sweet and spicy with a touch of rum — this drink takes me to a warm kitchen filled with laughter, music and coffee. Children can enjoy this seasonal treat without the rum.

4 cups hot brewed double-strength coffee	Mix coffee with molasses in a saucepan. Stir while heating.
6 tbsp molasses	Make sure the molasses is dissolved and the coffee is very hot, but do not let it boil.
6 tbsp dark rum (optional)	Dark rum can be poured in each cup if desired, then add fresh coffee.
Small amount whipped cream	Top with whipped cream and nutmeg.
Pinch ground nutmeg	

Kanuck Koffee

Canada is known for the highest quality maple syrup. This sweet ingredient is blended with whiskey to create the ideal combination to enjoy while you're ice fishing.

30ml (1oz) pure maple syrup

30ml (1oz) Canadian whiskey

1 cup double-strength hot coffee

Whipped cream and maple topping

Combine syrup, whiskey and coffee in a preheated mug.

Garnish with whipped cream, maple syrup and a Canadian flag if desired.

Café d'Orange

Coffee and orange are complementary flavours. The sweetness of the orange liqueur tempers the dark coffee for a rich, tangy cocktail.

30ml (1oz) Cognac

30ml (1oz) Mandarin Napoleon

15ml (½oz) Cointreau

120ml (4oz) freshly brewed double-strength coffee

Small amount whipped cream

Pinch orange rind

Pour cognac and liquors into a heated brandy snifter.

Add hot coffee.

Top it with whipped cream and spirals of orange rind.

Café Royal

Nothing but coffee, brandy and sweetness go into this simple refreshment. Guests will feel like royalty when presented with steaming mugs of Café Royal.

360ml (12oz) double-strength brewed coffee

1 tsp white sugar

Dash of brandy

Fill mug two-thirds with coffee.

Hold a teaspoon over the coffee cup and place the sugar and brandy in the spoon.

Light the brandy.

Flames will burn off the spoon, then place sugar and brandy into the coffee.

Café Spice

Café Spice is a tasty melding of spices, liqueur and coffee — a little like a Sangria wine for winter, when we see rainfall for days, even weeks on end.

2 whole cloves	Place the cloves, cinnamon stick, sugar, and orange rind in a saucepan. Heat until sugar begins to dissolve. Add the brandy and orange liqueur and continue to heat. When hot, fill a large metal spoon with liquid and set it alight.
1 cinnamon stick	
1 tbsp brown sugar	
1 orange rind	
½ cup brandy	
30ml (1oz) orange liqueur	Once the contents of the spoon is flaming, pour it back into the saucepan. This will burn off any residual alcohol. Once the alcohol has burnt off, add the hot coffee and pour into preheated ceramic mugs. Garnish with lemon rind.
2 cups of double-strength coffee	
Lemon rind	

Recipe compliments of Danny Johns, WholeCup Coffee Consulting, *Barista* Trainer, US and International *Barista* Event Coordinator, Portland, Oregon, USA.

Café Mexican Chocolate

A delicious blend of sugars, brandy and spicy chocolate. This mixture can be made in advance and kept ready for guests.

1 tsp dark brown sugar

30ml (1oz) Mexican chocolate shavings

15ml (½oz) brandy

Double-strength brewed coffee

1 cinnamon stick

1 clove

30ml (1oz) coffee liqueur optional

Combine sugar, chocolate and brandy in a preheated Irish coffee glass.

Add the double-strength brewed coffee to the glass and mix well.

Garnish with a cinnamon stick and a whole clove.

Recipe compliments of Danny Johns, WholeCup Coffee Consulting, *Barista* Trainer, US and International *Barista* Event Coordinator, Portland, Oregon, USA.

B&B Iced Coffee

Brandy, Baileys and toddy coffee are used to make a refreshing cold coffee drink with a jolt. Effortless to prepare — and consume.

30ml (1oz) coffee brandy	Combine all the ingredients in an 'on the rocks' glass and mix well.
30ml (1oz) Baileys	Pour the mixture over the coffee ice cubes.
Chilled toddy coffee	Pour into glasses and serve.
Coffee ice cubes	

Recipe compliments of Danny Johns, WholeCup Coffee Consulting, *Barista* Trainer, US and International *Barista* Event Coordinator, Portland, Oregon, USA.

Shakerato

This classic coffee cocktail is whipped up in seconds. Friends and family will enjoy watching you prepare it. The froth rises to the top of the drink and softly greets your taste buds.

30ml (1oz) espresso or coffee of choice

1 tbsp liquid sugar

6 ice cubes

Put all the ingredients in a shaker and shake rapidly for 45 seconds.

Serve in a chilled champagne glass.

Garnish with a decorative stir stick.

For multiple drinks, increase the shaker size and multiply the ingredients by the number of servings.

Recipe compliments of Fritz Storm, World Champion *Barista* 2002, Denmark.

Iced Flavoured Coffee Toddy Martini

Espresso, double-strength coffee or toddy coffee can be used to prepare this signature drink. Elegant in martini glasses and ideal for Sunday brunch.

30ml (1oz) almond or hazelnut syrup

2 cups double-strength brewed coffee

½ cup fresh cold milk

Coffee ice cubes

Chocolate coffee beans or a mint sprig

Straws

Pour a small amount of flavoured syrup into a cocktail shaker.

Add the coffee and fresh cold milk.

Fill the shaker with coffee ice cubes and shake vigorously.

Pour into martini glasses and add a straw.

Garnish with chocolate coffee beans or a mint sprig.

Frozen Coffee Cooler

This recipe is versatile because the guest is not limited to one flavour. There is a multitude of taste sensations to choose from.

60ml (2oz) vanilla syrup

60ml (2oz) any flavour syrup, your choice

2 espressos

60ml (2oz) fresh cream or chantilly

720ml (24oz) crushed or cubed ice

Blend all ingredients until smooth.

Serve in a martini or tall, decorative glass.

Recipe compliments of *barista* Sandy Hon of Java Jazz, Kansas City, USA.

Sweet Success

The *barista* unites espresso and sweetened condensed milk for stylish creamy coffee cocktails. Quite scrumptious at any time of day or night.

2 espressos

30ml (1oz) sweetened condensed milk

60ml (2oz) of full cream

Zest of one orange

Place all ingredients into a stainless steel martini shaker.

Shake for 45 seconds.

Strain and pour into tall apéritif glassware.

Add orange zest.

Variation: for a sweeter drink, use coconut milk in place of half and half.

Sprinkle with toasted coconut flakes.

Recipe compliments of *barista* Sandy Hon, Java Jazz, Kansas City, Missouri, USA.

Frappé Coffee

The French word for blending comes into its own when mixing chilled coffee with ice-cream. Prepare multiple drinks in one go for a group of customers or friends.

240ml (8oz) chilled toddy or double-strength coffee

1 cup flavoured ice-cream

1 tbsp vanilla extract or syrup

Place all ingredients in a blender.

Blend the mixture until smooth and serve in a tall glass.

Garnish with a colourful straw.

Frappé Mocha

Similar to the Frappé Coffee but comes with a chocolate twist. This is a crowd pleaser that no one turns down. Have as much fun making this as you would drinking it.

240ml (8oz) chilled double-strength coffee

2 scoops chocolate ice-cream

30ml (1oz) chocolate syrup

Chocolate shavings, cherries or chocolate cookie straw (optional)

Place all ingredients in a blender, and blend until smooth.

Pour into chilled tall glasses.

Garnish with chocolate shavings, a cherry or a chocolate cookie straw.

Mocha Mint Frappé

Toddy coffee is made in advance and kept fresh in the refrigerator. Also good is freshly prepared espresso spiked with the freshness of mint.

1 cup chilled toddy coffee

1 cup chocolate ice-cream

30ml (1oz) mint syrup

Chocolate shavings

Mint sprig

Place all the ingredients in a blender and blend until smooth.

Pour the mixture into a tall glass.

Garnish with chocolate shavings and a mint sprig.

Espresso Malt

Melt the chocolate to the rim of the glass and use a toothpick to create designs. It's artistic, easy and fun.

60ml (2oz) vanilla syrup	Place all ingredients in a blender and blend until smooth.
1 tbsp vanilla extract	Pour the mixture into a tall glass.
180ml (5oz) vanilla ice-cream	Garnish the drink with a colourful straw and a tall spoon.
3 tbsp malt powder	
60ml (2oz) espresso	

Recipe compliments of *barista* Stefanie Raymond of *Barista*'s Daily Grind, Kearny, Nebraska, USA.

Sweet Banana Frappé

Imagine banana, chocolate and coffee
blended together to create an elixir
that most can't resist.

2 cups chilled toddy coffee

1 cup chocolate ice-cream

1 ripe banana

Chocolate shavings

Place all ingredients in a blender and blend until smooth.

Pour into an 'on the rocks' glass.

Garnish with chocolate shavings.

Emerald Coffee Cooler

The Emerald Coffee Cooler has creative combinations of ingredients that one may not think of joining in a glass. Here's one you will enjoy.

240ml (8oz) heavy whipping cream

4 tsp sugar

½ cup jellied mint leaves

2 tsp caramel sauce

2 tsp cinnamon syrup

120ml (4oz) espresso

Mint leaves

1 strawberry

Whip cream and sugar in a blender until thickened but pourable. Thin the jellied mint leaves in a blender and fold into the cream. Pour mint cream into four pint-size glasses and chill. Dissolve the caramel sauce and syrup into the espresso.

Insert a small funnel through the chilled cream mixture to the bottom of the glass. Slowly pour the espresso mixture into the funnel while lifting it. Warm liquid will stay in the bottom of the cup as the chilled mint cream mixture rises, creating two distinct layers and colours. Garnish the drink with mint leaves and a sliced strawberry if desired.

Recipe compliments of *barista* Mark Pfaff, Jasper's Coffee House, Federal Way, WA, USA.

Index

Acknowledgements

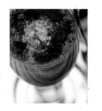

This book is dedicated to my mom who has always inspired me, my husband Danny who supports, encourages and "puts up with me", my many coffee friends, who inspire, motivate and heckle me, the coffee farmers and the baristas who support quality coffee. Special thanks to Nathalie for her designer eye, the food stylist, Anke, who tasted every drink I made, Alfred for his kindness and Nicky for her perseverance. Also, thanks to Filtron; Blendtec Blenders; Solis Grinder; Zoka Coffee Roaster; La Marzocco; and John Lear and Michael Beyer of Gourmet Coffees.